SECRET PICTURE SEARCH

RED
BIRD
PRESS

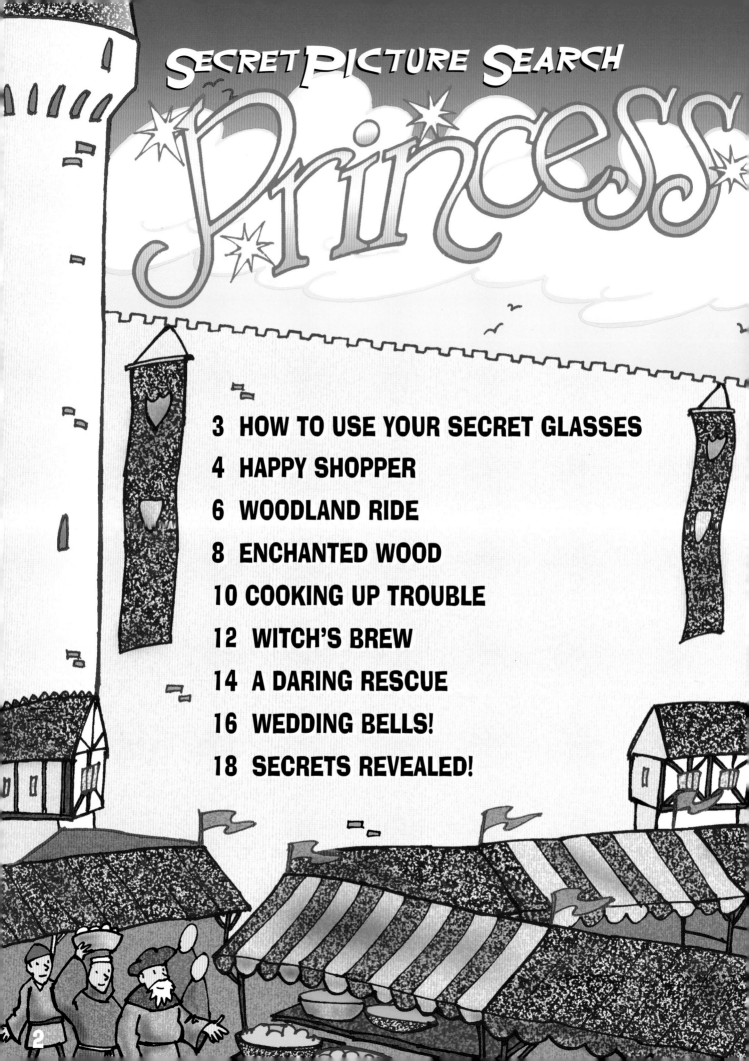

SECRET PICTURE SEARCH

Princess

HOW TO USE YOUR

SECRET GLASSES

Look at each scene and read the story. Put on your Secret Glasses to reveal the hidden characters – there are over 100 to find in this book. Can you find them all? You can check the answers on pages 18 and 19.

It's a sunny day in the market and Princess Victoria is shopping for supper. The cook has given her a big shopping list. The Princess's magical playmates have come along too – they want to

4

have some fun! Put on your Secret Glasses and join in the shopping spree. Aren't Victoria's tiny friends funny? Can you find the lazy one? What things have they hidden?

After the shopping, Princess Victoria goes for an afternoon ride with her boyfriend, Prince David. Victoria's pony, Sparkle, loves to gallop through the enchanted wood. Be careful, Victoria, don't

ride off too far! Using your Secret Glasses, can you see any woodland creatures? How many can you find? Are Victoria's friendly elves and pixies still following her?

Oh, dear! The Princess is lost – she rode off too quickly. But, hello, who is this? The old lady tells the Princess not to worry and offers her a snack back at her tumbledown cottage. "Don't go" plead the

tiny folk. They know that this is the wicked witch of the wood and she will be up to no good! How many winged fairies are keeping a watchful eye on Victoria? Use your Secret Glasses to find out.

Back in the castle kitchen, Prince David and the King are worried that Victoria hasn't come home. Where can she be? Her little friends know what has happened, where she is and what danger

she is in. They must raise the alarm. "Hurry up, Prince David, Victoria is in danger!" This way, everyone – put on your Secret Glasses and join the rescue party.

Oh no! Poor Princess Victoria has been locked up in a rusty cage. The old witch does not want Victoria to marry Prince David – the witch wants to become queen herself! Now she is mixing up a

magic potion to make her young and lovely again. "Soon I will be beautiful once more," she cackles as all her creatures gather round. Be careful where you look!

Suddenly there's a loud noise outside. Prince David and the tiny army crash through the heavy oak door to overpower the witch and save the Princess. "No more of your wicked ways!" they chuckle.

"You'll never become queen! Stay here and don't ever trouble us again." Put on your Secret Glasses. Are you ready for the biggest party ever? It looks as if Victoria's triumphant army is!

Princess Victoria and Prince David are married. At the Grand Ball, when the music starts, they are the first to dance. The King and all the guests, especially Victoria's little friends, are

enjoying the celebration. Put on your Secret Glasses and join in the party. Can you see what fun they are having? Maybe some have had too much cake but it doesn't stop them dancing!

Princess SECRETS REVEALED!

How many hidden characters did you find? Look at these boxes to check and count them all. Use your Secret Glasses to see the magic total.

4 HAPPY SHOPPER

We all enjoy shopping in a busy marketplace where local people trade their goods. Some country markets in England are very old – existing even before Roman times.

10 COOKING UP TROUBLE

Cooking is very important in a big castle or a small house! Favorite recipes in medieval times included Stuffed Swan, Roast Pig, Venison Pie and Honey Pudding.

12 WITCH'S BREW

Secret potions using natural ingredients have long been used by herbalists all over the world. But beware, this is for experts only!

6 WOODLAND RIDE

Sadly, ancient woods are becoming rare. All over the world, woods and forests are being cut down to make way for new houses and roads. But trees are very important to us because they release oxygen into the air.

8 THE ENCHANTED WOOD

Getting lost in a deep, dark wood can be very scary. It is always best to go with an adult, stick to the path and to remember where you have been, so you can get back to safety.

14 A DARING RESCUE

Through the ages, heroic rescues have filled the pages of many a thrilling story, from the Bible to Star Wars. What is your favorite?

16 WEDDING BELLS!

Everyone enjoys a good party, and weddings are a great reason for celebrating. Weddings in some countries, such as India, can last up to ten days!

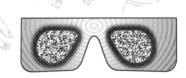